Stone
Bow
Prayer

Amy Uyematsu

Stone
Bow
Prayer

COPPER CANYON PRESS

Cover art: Alan Magee, *Convergence,* 2002, acrylic and oil on panel, 50" × 40". Courtesy of Forum Gallery, New York; private collection.

Copper Canyon Press is in residence at Fort Worden State Park in Port Townsend, Washington, under the auspices of Centrum Foundation. Centrum is a gathering place for artists and creative thinkers from around the world, students of all ages and backgrounds, and audiences seeking extraordinary cultural enrichment.

LIBRARY OF CONGRESS CATALOGING-IN-PUBLICATION DATA

Uyematsu, Amy.
Stone, bow, prayer / Amy Uyematsu.
    p.   cm.
ISBN 1-55659-221-3 (pbk.: alk. paper)
I. Title.
PS3571.Y66S76 2005
811'.54 — DC22

2004020188

COPPER CANYON PRESS
Post Office Box 271
Port Townsend, Washington 98368

www.coppercanyonpress.org

ACKNOWLEDGMENTS

Special thanks to Michelle Reed, Ann Colburn, Daria Donovan, Lee McCarthy, and always, friend and teacher Peter Levitt. I am also grateful for the many years of support from poet-editors Robert McDowell, Erick Chock, Darrell Lum, Mifanwy Kaiser, Jackson Wheeler, David Oliveira, Terry Wolverton, Dana Gioia, and Russell Leong. Finally, the unwavering love and enthusiasm of Raul Candido Contreras, Chris Tachiki, and Elsie Uyematsu help me believe.

The author has been inspired by Sam Hamill's work and vision — both as poet and founder of Copper Canyon Press as well as peace activist and organizer of Poets Against the War. Heartfelt thanks to Sam. Through his generous, attentive, and patient eye, this book evolved from earlier drafts.

Grateful acknowledgment is also made to the editors of the following publications, where these poems first appeared (some in slightly different versions):

Another City: Writing from Los Angeles — "Before"

APA Journal — "Song on a Chinese Plain"

Art/Life — "Palette," *"how close,"* "To Know Her," "Presence" (under the title "Old Monk")

Bakunin — "The Meaning of Zero: A Love Poem"

Bamboo Ridge Journal — "He Swears He Never Knew," "The Flowering Eye"

Bloomsbury Review — "A Practical Mom"

Beyond the Valley of the Contemporary Poets — "Unfinished Calculations"

Crab Orchard Review — "Storm"

88: A Journal of Contemporary American Poetry — "Sukoshi/Little Bites"

Gidra: The Twentieth Anniversary Edition — "He Built Her a Garden"

Grand Passion: The Poets of Los Angeles and Beyond — "Duet"

Kyoto Journal — "Inheritance"

Lucid Stone — "Balancing Stones"

Luna — "Purple like Iris," "Stone, Bow, Prayer"

Monolid — "Beyond Simple Counting"

Mountain Muse — "On Hummingbirds," "Winter Garden"

Paterson Literary Review — "A Gift of Iris in Winter: Improvisations"

Rattle — "1110 on My Transistor Dial"

So Luminous the Wildflowers: An Anthology of California Poets — "I'm Old Enough to Know Better"

Solo — "Always Eleven," "Heat," "Unexpected Passage"

Sonnets at Work — "Flavor of the Month"

Spillway — "Even Now," "Inside," "Autumn" (under the title "October")

Temple — "Looking"

What Book!? Buddha Poems from Beat to Hiphop — "Inside" ("lone pine"), "Tea"

Zyzzyva — "The Fold"

Sincere thanks to Sally McLaren, whose "Japanese Times of the Year" (*Kyoto Journal*, No. 42, 1999) supplied information about Japan's lunar calendar; month names and translations used as section titles in this collection are based on her article.

To my parents,
Elsie Shizuko Morita &
Francis Genichiro Uyematsu

*And what is the name of the month
that falls between December and January?*

Pablo Neruda,
The Book of Questions

*The poems in this volume have been organized into
twelve sections based on the ancient lunar calendar
of China. Dividing the year into 29- and 30-day
months, the calendar was adopted by Japan around
the seventh century A.D. and used until it was re-
placed by the Gregorian system, in 1873. Sections
have been named according to the early Japanese
lunar months.*

Contents

Stone
Bow
Prayer

1

Mutsuki Month of Friendly Harmony

Song on a Chinese Plain

A man remembers
bathing in a river
but wakes in this field of wind
hears the sound he once carried through water.

There are no eyes here
only arms set loose
and feet moving silent
in the yellow grass.

A girl rides in
on a blue-gray horse
the animal knows her small open hand
the dream she keeps to herself.

A stone reveals the ground's tremble
this long waiting for rain
the rustle our feet make
even when we leave.

The Earliest Sounds

water always water
Daria Donovan

seaborne we come,
each invisible
seed, still
as water suspended
in the warm dark body,
this silence,
a journey
      by water

long before
the first
breath, that small
wind bursting
      only water

before the hard-
earned immersion
into air &
the light that
intrudes inside
uneasy eyes
      this stillness

which encircles
a quiver
of cells, precious
fluid that cushions
every human

contortion
            always water

as limb buds
tremble
into fingers &
toes, no noise
as they twitch
& uncurl
            quiet water

whose music
we're unable to hear,
tiny ears
only skin
on each side
of the head
            no sound

until the world
enters, in its promise,
opening
the labyrinth,
unwinding each tunnel
of membrane & bone
            the first vibration

listened to,
here in the darkness,
this heart beating
just beyond
the caved wall,
insistent drumming
            that calls

Storm

after hearing "Monochrome,"
by the Kodō drummers

At first we hear nothing
    only the barest flicker
        of wrists and sticks appears

Then a flutter of sound
    coming closer together
        until everyone hears

This delicate drizzle
    pretending to lull us
        its liquid drone

Slowly swells to a clatter
    the hands moving now
        in frenzied precision

So unforgiving
    the staccato air
        its godly clamor

Drilling the ear
    then arms falling still
        the silence

That comes after rain
    and we never suspect
        how much heaven needs us

Sukoshi / Little Bites

call me
frivolous
I can look
for days
at that pale
green
cup

᠊᠊᠊

each rain-
drop grows
louder?
no, hear
the drown of
my heart

᠊᠊᠊

amazed
by one more
season, Mother's
string beans
so crispy
and sweet

᠊᠊᠊

the sound
of white moving

blue, a ripple
of one
awakened

~

you ask
the oak
I'll smell
the pine
our preference
becomes us

Duet

The first man is young and lean.
Black skin. Black baggy pants
and a pressed black T-shirt.
The only white — in his eyes
and short rolled cotton socks.
Color is chosen deliberately.
To illuminate the body, flash
from eyes to feet. He knows
his power over the crowd
that grows at Santa Monica Pier,
his body robotlike but smoother —
as an invisible thread of heat
enters his right hand and rises
to elbow, pulses
from shoulder to shoulder,
then vibrating out
the left wrist and fingers.
He doesn't even have to think —
just moves.

The second man can't stay away.
Every time the beat quickens,
this white man rushes over, stomping
the ground as fast as he can.
The audience buzzes
as if he can't hear. Saying he's crazy
or loaded, that he's slept in his clothes.
Jeans slipping down his thin, naked butt,
he keeps drumming his feet. The beat
shifts down and his hips sashay

in a lecherous bend
while the onlookers roar.

The white man lives under
the boardwalk. Listens to footsteps
overhead night and day,
falls asleep to the sound of waves.
No one talks to him anymore.
The young black man doesn't either
but won't stop him from moving closer,
their bodies almost touching.
Even when the audience laughs,
they'll dance all afternoon —
long after the crowd moves on.

2

Kisaragi Month of Putting On More Clothes

Looking

I've begun to study
how a woman can try
drawing attention
to her face
a slightly rosier shade
on her cheeks
real diamond earrings
a red silk scarf
draping the neck
covers the telltale
skin at the throat

there's the shattering
uncertain time
when a woman becomes unseen
when she can walk down a street
or enter a crowded bar
and not feel the heat of any man's stare
that radar which so often
unnerved her
probing and intruding
the inescapable
penetration
of his eye

it's the unannounced hour
when she first recalls
that dogs no longer sniff her
do not rush her
on instinct

lured by the unmistakable
odor of blood

such a woman may learn
she's been far too frivolous
even lately admits
how she misses
the embarrassment
of an occasional whistle
an undisguised leer
wishes she'd thanked every man
who took his sweet time
just to keep looking her way

Before

Such unwelcome commotion – how long the walk home, crying
after the other kids peek under my skirt, an echo of giggling. Then
louder the lure of sycamore and pine. That purple flowering on lacy
jacaranda and eucalyptus-filled skies whose perfume is always
dizzying and sweet. The surprise of sliding down poles at recess,
legs tightly entwined, pelvis against steel. What to call this
unexpected friction – still nameless between soft and hard, this secret
to repeat if no one's looking. The grip of Mr. Sato's hand when
I'm eleven, his fingers holding my hip bone for speechless seconds.
And I want to run away, unsure why he studies me so strangely.
Long before I lie awake in the dark – not knowing the words – as I
call on my hands to answer.

Always Eleven

is the one left behind
who's never asked to join
no secret pacts with
other little girls
who whisper
and shriek
giggling their way
through the teens

to not even notice
when my breasts
start changing
no tender instructions
from my photogenic mother
who doesn't want
to be reminded
or a father who stops
kissing me goodnight
without warning

I have to be told
to look at "them" bounce
through my thin cotton blouse
all the kids at recess
following my fat chest
as I'm rounding third base
how quickly
those well-meaning girls
rush up to hide me
everyone can see

so ready to advise
you better get a bra

I don't even make it
to June graduation
no time to recover
before the first spots of red

I'm told very little
as if one elastic belt
a napkin
and two safety pins
are sufficient induction

the next month is worse
when I'm away from home
on a Girl Scout campout
how can I know
the flow will thicken
still no female to turn to
afraid of the stains
that can bleed through
and show

never to be twelve
is to fill up with shame
to lie so far inside
the body a girl
can vanish
and no one will even
bother asking
where she's gone

He Swears He Never Knew

*To have the remembrance of what we were &
have to see what we've become – it's cruel – if
you were put to thinking up a refined torture
for a mentality such as ours carnate like us you
would think up exactly what happens to us –*

Albert Saijo, "Aging"

He's only forty-two and just a few pounds over
not enough to explain
the tiny twin bulges which poke through his T-shirts
the nipples sneaking through the thin cotton knits
he used to wear on weekends
lately his eyes are his worst enemies
no longer hurtling into that hungry race for titillation
as he finds himself staring
at all recognizable shapes of the masculine
back and forth from the tanned bared chests
to the sad, sagging torsos
noticing for the first time in his life
every old forgotten guy at the gym
these tragedies who quietly surround him
as if nothing at all is wrong with the picture
the unmistakable breasts hanging from the trim
sixty-year-old swimmers to the fat-whiskered walruses,
who somehow sit naked and unbothered
in the sauna and locker room, everywhere he looks
these traitor tits not to mention other parts
that have fallen unmentionable inches
he keeps catching glimpses of his own
pale flesh in full-length mirrors
reassured by muscles only beginning to droop
over the breastbone and ribs

small consolation but he'll grab whatever he can
in this speeding blind zone this old man's world
he swears he never saw coming.

Even Now

a reply to the question,
"Can you still be hip at 50?"

Hip out, girl
curl a whistle
in your strut
make that riff
a little rough
hang out your flaunt
flap and feather
just a whiff
this side of shy
enough to atomize
the breeze
that eases you
back in

      yeah
it's easy still
just rip, girl
the same old
hide and tease
slide that squeeze
into his shaker
tweak a tender
to his sigh
and always
let him
woo the hum
inside your tangle
till you swoosh
and wing him by

3

Yayoi Month of Renewed Growth

The Meaning of Zero: A Love Poem

And is where space ends
called death or infinity?

Pablo Neruda,
The Book of Questions

A mere eyelid's distance between you and me.

It took us a long time to discover the number zero.

John's brother is afraid to go outside.
He claims he knows
the meaning of zero.

I want to kiss you.

A mathematician once told me you can add infinity
to infinity.

There is a zero vector, which starts and ends
at the same place, its force
and movement impossible
to record with
rays or maps or words.
It intersects yet runs parallel
with all others.

A young man I know
wants me to prove
the zero vector exists.
I tell him I can't,
but nothing in my world
makes sense without it.

Permutations

⤶

stone in water
growing
still

water in stone
still
growing

⤶

in the I whose eye
in the eye what sky
in the sky where's I

⤶

ow – ow – ow – ow – howl
ow – ow – ow – ow – owl
ow – ow – ow – ow – wow
ow – ow – ow – ow – bow

⤶

the nothingness of all
the whole in the hole

how perfect a fit

When Geometry Gets Mixed Up with God
and the Alphabet

Every time he writes "angel" she puts a big red circle
around it, not round like a halo but cranky
and shrill with her thick felt-tip pen,
just for misspelling "angle" again,
as she takes a point off here, another point there,
until he's down to a lousy C-plus.

She's gotta be the pickiest teacher Joey's ever had
'cuz she makes them spell the words
like it's some dumb English class
and a sin to write "slop" for "slope"
or "rumbas" for "rhombus." She expects
him to give reasons and claims "just because
it looks that way" doesn't make it true.
It's usually Joey who blurts out,
"What's the point
if I can figure it out in my head?" –
but she'll throw him that look
that makes the whole room quiet
without saying one word.

Joey will never admit it to his best friend Andrew,
who sits in the corner and counts
the number of tiny holes in the ceiling tiles,
once up to 2,407 when the bell rang,
that geometry is his favorite class
even though he hates the homework.
Sometimes he'll figure out all the problems she assigns
but will never hold up his hand to answer

because Andrew and he can't stand
those show-offs who always wave their arms
like they want everyone
to know who's smartest.

Some days she puts on that crazy smile of hers
and starts asking questions like *How do we know*
a line is straight or *Do we believe that*
between any two points there's always one more?
Joey doesn't doubt that numbers can get bigger
and never stop, but he's fascinated
by the idea of infinity shrinking, too.
Once she asked if his class ever stops to wonder
why Egyptians chose triangles for their pyramids,
even believed these three-sided shapes held
secret powers. Joey joins in
as the kids laugh and roll their eyes
with that oh-no-here-she-goes-again sigh,
but lately he wishes they'd shut up a minute
so he can let his mind zoom
to a space he can't see,
where ocean meets sky and lines can curve.

Joey might even break his rule
about homework and answer her question —
"What geometric shape pleases you most?" —
because there's no doubt in Joey's mind
that circles are the best things ever invented.
He even wishes he could meet the first genius
who drew a circle in the sand;
though the more Joey thinks about it,
circles didn't have to be invented —
from the moon and the sun

to eyeballs, round stones, oranges,
humans have always seen circles —
from the minute they wake up
to when they go to sleep, circles.

And Joey can't explain
why circles make him feel happy —
but he's glad she's taught him
about "concentric" circles,
pondering one inside another
inside another without end.

The Invention of Mathematics

A man who is not somewhat of a poet can never be a mathematician.

Karl Weierstrass, German
mathematics teacher

/ one

one is the only true number
the I in the eye
each baby the god
in a mother's sigh

/ two

after the number two there was no stopping
troubles blossoming
in geometric progression
two to tango
and two required for murder and war
Doris Day singing
love me or leave me
and the tragic lob
of my nervous girlheart
th-thump, th-thump
she already knew
that deafening silence
when the call goes unanswered
th-thump, th-thump
with its inevitable
downbeat on two

/ seven

how could 7 not be lucky for me
with four 7s in my phone number
the year I was born 47 reversing perfectly
to 74 when I gave birth to my son
whose sign is in July, the 7th month,
like my mother and father,
two stubborn Leos in their vigorous 70s

I'm thankful to be
a Saturday matinee kid
raised somewhere between
Snow White and the 7 Dwarfs,
7 Brides for 7 Brothers,
and Kurosawa's heroic
7 Samurai

Japan has 7 gods of fortune
with the only woman
being the goddess Benten,
ruler of the sea,
a lute-shaped biwa in her arms
she's the guardian
of literature and song

and 7 syllables, a gift of blood
the lines of a tanka swinging
to 5-7-5-7-7 rhythms
the tradition of haiku parties
jamming long into night
only natural I'd arrive
with a poem in my hand

/ irrational

how fitting there are even eccentrics
among the legions of numbers
so stubborn they defy
any notion of orderly arrangement
numbers like *pi* or the *square root of two*
whose decimal translations
burst all reasonable boundaries
the ever-erratic digits
never repeating
no end in sight to their
unwinding names

and I have to admit
I wave the banner
of every so-called irrational woman
who can juggle five things in each hand
a skill little girls learn by nine or ten
while our somewhat dazed
and mystified mates
stand by in hopeless wonder

/ the imaginary number i

my students don't get the joke
after all, every number is imaginary
even those we count out
as beads and stones and miles to the sun

I tell them about some nameless
mathematicians who nobody paid

much attention to
always gazing at stars

these early oddballs and nerds
locked in their rooms
pondering pages of silly calculations
as if all life depended on them

until someone yelled *i*
let's make up a new number
defined as the square root
of negative one

blasting open the infinite
which no one can see
able to chart arrow to bull's-eye
through windstorm and breeze

A Practical Mom

can go to Bible study every Sunday
and swear she's still not convinced,
but she likes to be around people who are.
We have the same conversation
every few years — I'll ask her if she stops
to admire the perfect leaves
of the Japanese maple
she waters in her backyard,
or tell her how I can gaze for hours
at a desert sky and know this
as divine. Nature, she says,
doesn't hold her interest. Not nearly
as much as the greens, pinks, and grays
of a Diebenkorn abstract, or the antique
Tiffany lamp she finds in San Francisco.
She spends hours with her vegetables,
tasting the tomatoes she's picked that morning
or checking to see which radishes are big enough to pull.
Lately everything she touches bears fruit,
from new-green string beans to winning
golf strokes, glamorous hats she designs and sews,
soaring stocks with their multiplying shares.
These are the things she can count in her hands,
the tangibles to feed and pass on to daughters
and grandchildren who can't keep up with all
the risky numbers she depends on, the blood-sugar counts
and daily insulin injections, the monthly tests
of precancerous cells in her liver and lungs.
She's a mathematical wonder with so many calculations
kept alive in her head, adding and subtracting
when everyone else is asleep.

Unfinished Calculations

How true is the line that keeps threading its way through,
too thin to cipher and with no start or end

when did I first hear a voice that keeps humming in my ear
when does a kiss weigh more than a fist, the kiss outlast the scar

is forgiveness always less than the magnitude of rage

after so many days of walking, what roads does the foot remember

how hard must wings push to lift up the body
how much rain to drown out the clamor of the mind

can anyone measure the diameter of want, the exponential distortion
of the glutted or starving eye

how many times must the human heart break

what is the sound of a singular stone,
spiraling into the center of the pond
where it ripples the surface in concentric circles,
each one drawn into the water's stillness

if each baby begins with one billion brain cells, how many
electrical signals sent out in the dark will be answered,
how many more neurons will die

how slim are the odds that one shall paint, another shall dance,
whose unexpected orbits keep intersecting mine

what is the slope of this spine I lean on, the arc of a lover's arm
how soon before the wrinkles on my neck cannot be smoothed with cream
why does the distance between us keep shifting
what is the meaning of one

how many pine needles can sweeten an entire forest
how wide does the sky open or close each time someone prays

what unproven dimension makes God as close as the wind which keeps
stirring my hair, is that why I listen
to the rustling of leaves

how deep is the garden where this heartroot descends

4

Uzuki Month of
the Rabbit

Inheritance

You come to me now, my Japanese
grandmothers, not as ghosts nor through
dream, but here in the body of this unlikely
woman named Ruby Odell, who delights in
things we call "very old."

I recognize the pastels in this woman's scarf,
the predominance of pale apricot pink,
waves of jade and slate in the grainy silk,
three surprising curves of persimmon revealing
an eye that's unmistakably Japanese —
the impulse toward heat
when feelings are muted.

∽

In the faded photo, two girls sleep under one
cotton quilt, their heads close enough
to know each other's dreams. Strange
that it should make me think of us, two sisters
who used to share the same room, now so long
grown up, each taking our secrets
lifetimes away to new cities, new beds,
while a father we hardly see still interrupts
our conversations — like something unfinished
that won't leave us alone.

∽

The doll is carefully wrapped in red tissue paper.
I don't expect the young boy, dressed in his best
kimono, a blue and white obi tied snugly at the hips.

His small open hands are still raised,
as if he's just released something precious,
watching it fly slowly away, no sound
of breath from his open mouth.

⤚

Like the woman in Kunisada's prints
who carefully brushes on powder,
reddens her lips, fastens the loose threads
of hair with black lacquer pins,
her gaze never wavering from the bedroom mirror,
I hold this comb carved from pine,
its teeth sturdy and even after so many years,
and remember the premise of evening routine,
my freshly washed hair, a luster like silk —
how slowly fingers could glide through
the heavy strands. Even tonight I carry
my wooden comb, as if there'll be an unexpected
meeting, a dinner invitation, as if I'll need
to comb my hair for you.

What Doesn't Die

*And after all, we've been here ever since the
beauty of the universe needed someone to see it.*
Eduardo Galeano, *Walking Words*

I come from a tribe who knows its world from seeing.
We don't talk as much as our noisier neighbors,
like the tribe to the west who lives in red houses,
or the birds who perch outside our windows and notice
how quietly we eat our evening meal.
We're not like those irrepressible romantics, lavishing
the kiss in song. Even saying "I love you" can be impossible.

The eyes passed on to me could only belong to an island
of such rare beauty, an accident of rock and fire rising out of
the cold Pacific to become this land grown lush with green,
still constantly fed from rain and stream and ocean mist.
Around any curve of our coastline there's a pine forest
or waterfall, a sculptured cliff or cypress to greet us.
For as long as we can remember, everywhere we looked
was stunning. Small wonder that our eyes
narrowed permanently, turning up at the ends as we laugh
with delight. Only natural that my tribe would name
our members stone, valley, river, mountain, tree.

Where I come from the vocabulary for love is far too shy.
But beauty is another matter — from *bijin* courtesans, timeless
on woodblock prints, to *kirei*, pretty arrangements of camellia
and moss. A red maple is *migoto,* while a lovely lacquer tray,
not from nature, is *kareina.* The burst of spring cherry blossoms,
that glorious peach and pink, is *subarashii,* while we call
quieter beauty *shibui,* like a pale green teacup or the muted

blue lilac of a silk kimono. And *wabi-sabi* embraces that tiny flaw
and odd imperfection, wedding radiance to the most ordinary.

The body withers, but beauty — ever generous — satisfies
that exquisite ache to be tickled and tantalized,
always feeding the unfinished urge to see her
for one more luxurious second.

Inside

based on photographs from Rural Japan:
Radiance of the Ordinary

/ afloat

two boats with no riders
still moving on water
the hulls barely touching
each with a single oar
safely propped
so it won't fall

/ lotus leaves

close into themselves
at night

on their wide folded backs
water beads

inside, their sleeping
flowers

/ inside

do the carp
just below the water's stillness
see the pines

/ fall daikon

just pulled from the soil
these pungent roots
hang from bamboo poles
their white tubed bodies
bend as if slightly aroused

each ripe radish will
be drenched
in salt
then eaten raw
all winter

/ lone pine

ancient tree
with so many tongues

how long this throated stem
this stillness before rain

5

Satsuki Month of Planting
Rice Shoots

The Fold

Only a well-trained eye
can spy a certain vulnerability
in women like me — to have
double lids makes the face
more Western, suggests the Eurasian,
may even determine a young girl's fate.

Even simpler than reducing a nose
or rewiring a smile: it takes
one quick hour to reshape the eye,
just a tiny incision,
bigger and rounder eyes growing more
common on both Pacific shores.

As long as most Asian women are born
missing this extra feature, doctors
like my uncle will always have business,
five lid operations a week,
five times $3,500 will make everyone happy,
a popular gift from parents to daughters.

Maybe I was luckier than others,
an infant female with wide-lidded eyes,
the family so pleased,
but I remember days in my teens
when I'd wake with a lid gone,
much too embarrassed to face the outside.

How eagerly I learned the cosmetic secret
shared between young Asian women —
a thin sliver of Scotch tape to glue
that painful crease into my skin,
then a fine-tipped brush to paint
a black line over the shiny strip.

No one showed me the ancient woodblocks —
Utamaro beauties enchanting men
with their eyes; no one told me
a postwar history — Japan losing face
and Asian eyes growing shamefully small
during the American occupation.

In total surrender, a Singapore doctor
invented the *Bookoochai* method,
named after him, to re-form
the lid, cutting a false fold
to imitate the more desirable
white, feminine eye.

It's hard to admit I've held those with
eye jobs in some disdain, having enjoyed
my slight advantage over the other
desperate girls, all of us vying
for Asian boyfriends who rank us
no more than second best.

It's been easier for me —
growing up, I was never called
"dime-slots" or taunted
with "How can you see?" —
though little kids would stare
or pull their eyes up tight and grin.

Simple Division

My history echoes
from small diameters —

120,000 issei and nisei
divided among 7 states

equals 10 barbed-wire
desert prison camps.

Desert Camouflage

for Jiro Morita

Grandpa was good at persuading the others
after the official evacuation orders.
Detained at Tulare Assembly Center,
he was the voice of reason among his angry friends,
raising everyone's spirits
when he started the morning exercise class.

Some issei said Grandpa couldn't be trusted —
after all, hadn't he volunteered
to fight in World War I?
And why did he speak better English
or brag that he was already a U.S. citizen
when the government denounced them as aliens?

At Gila, when nobody was willing
to make camouflage netting the military needed,
only Grandpa could talk them into it.
How many American soldiers would ever suspect
the netting protecting them was sewn by issei
whose faces could never be camouflaged?

I'm Old Enough to Know Better

To recognize that stupid smile
just before he asks,
"Do you teach the Korean class?"
He thinks he's getting one step closer
in the friendly nods we namelessly
exchange at work.
"I'm not Korean, I'm Japanese."
I wait to see how he'll react,
watching his half-open
mouth as he fumbles for words
and hoping he suffers
just a little embarrassment;
but just my luck,
he's an unconscious
stockpile of insults —
"Well, I'm just a round-eye,"
and he walks off grinning,
not even suspecting what
damage he's done for all
the "round-eyes" of this world.

It's my own fault
for trusting a town
where Asian faces are almost
as common as hearing Spanish,
and it surely feels safe enough
to walk on hip San Vicente
among those who love sushi,
dig yoga and Zen.

But I'm way too old
not to have seen the next one
coming, only two weeks later.
Three guys in suits, maybe tourists,
one looks at me as if we've met before.
Just as we pass
on that Brentwood sidewalk,
he leans toward me,
beaming, in broken English—
"Oriental massage, good."
The sad truth is,
he meant it
as a compliment.

Flavor of the Month

a reply to "Why Asian Guys Are on a Roll,"
Newsweek, *February 21, 2000*

is soy sauce served with a Tae Kwon Do twist.
America's newest hunks are Asian—
from Chow Yun-Fat to Yahoo's Jerry Yang,
they're no longer the dateless wimps and nerds
who watched their traitor women dance away.
No, who'd have guessed that brains and commitment
would become a sexy commodity,
or that smooth, gold- and tawny-colored skin bears
a sweeter scent and glistens in the sun.
The eyes which were once so sneaky and vile
laugh and disarm with dark intelligence.
Who can resist these clean-cut Romeos,
Mifune-like warriors, raven-haired studs
who still adore Mom—the secret is out.

1110 on My Transistor Dial

Shoo-bop, shoo-bop, my baby,
shoo-bop, shoo-bop

Barbara Lewis, "Hello Stranger"

No other station but 1110 AM
came to my adolescent rescue,
saving me from bubblegum pop tunes,
lovesick melodies, corn-syrup thick,
dance beats that couldn't find a rhythm
in that trite, too-white music
played by too many classmates
who acted like they liked me
but never asked me home.

I was destined to croon to a cooler sound – R&B,
that toe-tappin' hip-shakin' dance-until-you-drop
premium octane soul music, unmistakable in origin,
its spontaneous combustions from Chicago
to Harlem, Atlanta to Detroit and L.A.
It was the age of hi-fi 45s,
seven-inch platters whose integrity
was indelibly marked in their black
weathered grooves. Two dimes could buy
a hot dog, one nickel a pack of gum,
and my 50¢ weekly allowance enough
to build an impressive record collection –
Mary Wells and Marvin Gaye no more important
than the Dells, the Shirelles, or Shep
and the Limelites of "Daddy's Home" fame.
I was a sucker for romance in a cha-cha beat –
Billy Stewart wooing me with

"I Do Love You" or Dionne Warwick's
tearful reminder to "Walk On By."

On late Saturday nights kids from nearby
Rosemead and Whittier, all the way to Riverside,
Oxnard, and Chula Vista, would call up
Huggy Boy, Art Laboe, Wolfman Jack
with oldies dedications: *To Rosie from Chuckles;*
To Jesse, on our one-year; To Hector in 'Nam.
I eavesdropped along with thousands of other
love-starved regulars, all of us with nobody
special to send a song to over the airwaves.

It was no accident that every Buddhahead teen I met
was also listening to Motown, doo-wop, and funk—
the same music we played in basement socials at my all-Japanese
Presbyterian church was heard at Buddhist teen camps
high in the San Bernardino Mountains; the clean-cut boys
who drove up from Long Beach with their latest 45s
danced to the same beat as my rowdy Hollywood cousins.
This was the sixties, when there was nothing strange
about my being J-A in a small Wasp town, listening
to Chicanos phoning in dedications to a faceless deejay
named Huggy Boy, ethnicity unknown, who played
nothing but black and brown soul.

Today's paper announcing KRLA's "swan song"
reads too much like an obituary, including a color
publicity shot of Huggy Boy at the mike,
white-haired and wrinkled but still spinning
the "Duke of Earl" and "Sad Girl." Never disappointing
his fans, Huggy Boy ended his final fourteen-hour stint
with East L.A.'s Thee Midniters' "That's All."

It was the perfect ending—Little Willie G. promising,
"I can only give you love that lasts forever"—
this music I danced to just before the lights came on.

On November 29, 1998, Dick "Huggy Boy"
Hugg gave his last broadcast on Los Angeles
radio station KRLA, which changed to talk-
radio format.

6

Minazuki Waterless Month

Heat

It is still not summer
but it's too hot to sleep.
The same bird screeches
just outside our bedroom window.
Both of us recognize its cry,
that insistent chirping which kept us
awake so many nights last summer.
Has it already been one year
since you said you were leaving me?
You wonder out loud whether the bird
flew north or south for the winter.
It's just our luck
that blind, stubborn instinct leads
this noisy bird to our backyard,
to nest in its one lonely tree.

I nestle my head between
your shoulder and chest,
the place I can still keep
returning to safely,
but I have to position
my hands to my side,
or stretch an arm out
motionless across your body.
How well you've trained me
in the art of intimate distance.

Even when we wrestle and play
like lovers about to make love,
you hold down my hands so they won't

stray too close. It's not been easy,
your tenderness demanding
its own uncertain geography,
so when you slide your fingers
along my cheekbones
or stroke my hair,
I can't let myself get too aroused.

The bird won't stop squawking
but you're falling asleep anyway.
Lying next to you, I try
not to think too hard,
the bird shrill and tireless
through the long night.

Palette

I

She can't stop seeing the remarkable hues:
green calcite — that delicate jade
in its crystalline body, with rings
of lime, olive, maidenhair fern,
and Pacific seaweed.

Threading its base are tinctured veins
of brown and gold, birthmarks
from a random union of soil and sand
with rain and wind, ancient mutations.

She slides her hands over the cool green,
surprised that the coarse upper surface
is pale as frosted glass.

Floating inside are blossoms, tiny
brushstrokes of raspberry and tea rose,
below them some barely visible
clusters of purple — petals, perhaps,
or ocean coral still clinging to stone.

II

If only he watched
the way light and shadow are drawn to her breast,
delighting at the darkening areola
or the pink glow of skin just emerging
from waters still warm.

Will he ever really enter that cave
whose colors he's never likened
to blood's crimson mysteries,
the lush purples of birth?

When his fingers touch her
he doesn't watch her pelvis rising,
flesh glistening in the half-lit room;
he holds his lids shut,
forgets he once said
enchantment—
all his pretty painted words
betrayed again.

On Hummingbirds

Small bird with largest of hearts
in the family of winged animals
twelve hundred sixty beats every minute
twelve hundred sixty contractions –

and me with this heart flutter
unable to sleep
arms pressed tight against ribs.

II

This unnatural death —
when our animal scent still fills my bed
and, unprepared, my body
isn't ready to go into hiding.
But I am startled, twice
in barely two weeks
by these men I seem to lure
toward me, even now
when I can't see them coming.
There is something that remains
of our sex, a mysterious
odor that keeps rising from my skin —

like a dead hummingbird, once worn
around the neck in a tiny bag —
to give the wearer power.

He Built Her a Garden

One arching pine
two plum trees whose dark
purple leaves startle
the blankness of pale
brick walls —
a Japanese garden
in the back of their monotone
two-bedroom tract.

His daily tending
to its care
gentle tug of weeds
steadfastly arranging
the balance of stone and green —
a love poem to her.

But she was more flash
and articulation
and as her desperation
spoke volumes
he held his
own symmetry
moving silent things.

Now the plum leaves
brittle and brown
the garden remains —
an intruding quiet
that won't leave
her alone.

how close
the sound
of a river
gone

rich waters
that used
to rush
through the dark

a roar
held still
within
these thighs

voice
of infinite size
its unfinished
declaration

oh sweet
thrush
of longheld
words

who hears
the song
from the body's
dry mouth

oh heart
at the river's
end
who listens

7

Fumitsuki   Month of
Writing Poetry

Purple like Iris

after Jack Micheline's "Poem"
("I chose the whippoorwill")

I chose Cisco Kid, Tonto, and men dressed in black.
I cheered the loudest when the Indians attacked.
I chose loners, despising cliques at every age
but secretly hoping one day I'd get picked.

I chose revolution, not evolution.
I carried the *Red Book, Soul on Ice,* quoted from
Paolo Freire's *Pedagogy of the Oppressed.*
I knew the meaning of dialectical materialism.
Once I held my husband hostage for having no opinion.
Once a lover who wronged me said I take no prisoners.
I took sides like a junkie until I could see
they both cared about winning no matter the cost,
and when I chose to give up the battle,
a voice inside was still calling my name.

I always chose the romantic ending,
listened to torch songs long before
I'd ever died of longing.
I took my cues from the moon.
I chose saxophone and cha-cha, sipped Scotch
on the rocks, lounged
in the shade of June afternoons
slowly chewing the skin of a Japanese plum.
I chose purple for my bridesmaids
when the custom was pastel.
I wanted the alchemy of two hearts
but kept ending up with just one.

I chose "That's not fair" as my stubborn refrain.
The sky would rise bluer than gorgeous,
just to jeer me on.

I chose the wisdom of woman,
Mom over Dad even when she hurt him,
all the mothers of soldiers who never come back,
and the grandma who made my favorite rice balls
though she forgot to add wine to sweeten the vinegar.
How much I've relied on the kindred blessings
of goddess, witch, and crone.

I chose stone over grass, fish over bear.
Trusted hands that can make things grow
from cotton, clay, and seed.
I chose poetry because she spoke to me
so lovingly, the way my whole world
quieted to hear.

Tea

for Thich Nhat Hanh

How many years of suffering
revealed in hands like his
small and deliberate as a child's

The way he raises them
from his lap, grasps the teacup
with sure, unhurried ease

Yet full of anticipation
for what he will taste in each sip
he drinks as if it's his first time

Lifts the cup to his mouth,
a man who's been practicing all his life,
each time tasting something new.

The Weight of Nothing

to end with nothing is something
Suvan Geer

or to rephrase a popular Billy Preston song,
"somethin' from nothin' is somethin'"

I

everyone loves
the disappearing
coin. a bird pulled from
an empty hat. the comfort of
trusting a magician's hands.
when we know we'll get some-
thing from what
he takes away.

II

the student's assignment—
concentrate on nothing
for fifteen minutes a day.
she tries to empty her head
but can't figure out how.
after all, she doesn't know what
nothing sounds or looks like,
and the teacher won't give
the slightest clue. yet
she's got a good hunch
the exercise might quiet
all that shriek and clatter
trapped between her ears.
so like a good pupil,

she devotes an entire year
searching for nothing.
some days she's as still
as a stone, but can't
escape the distractions
of river and wind,
footsteps approaching,
birds calling in the trees
overhead. or closing
her eyes, she'll focus
on a cloudless blue sky.
pillows and planes and purple
sunsets keep interrupting.
she silently repeats words
like *ocean* or *why,*
chants sounds that dwell
low in her throat
like *maah* and *uhmm.*
at year's end her teacher
asks if she's found nothing.
she tells him she's found
everything but nothing.
he smiles, *you're closer*
than you think. now
try for twenty minutes.

III

we've all seen them —
looking at their empty
outstretched palms,
and we're fooled, thinking
about what isn't there.

sighing, they marvel
at all they've held in those hands,
their history revealed
in the thickened joints,
the full weight of their desire—
even now, incredible
hands still opening
and grasping
when there's nothing to keep.

    IV

without my friend Nothing
on the page, I'd never have to write
another poem. but Nothing waits
here, waving me on, inviting me
to rap and rant, pray, sing, testify
what is, was, could, and always will be.
I greet all that's coming,
contained as sheer breath
into word, born
to crave and engrave the emptiness
that Nothing can't stop giving.

8

Hazuki Month of Falling Leaves

Listen

What rush of wind stirs
         so many broad leaves
of that giant magnolia
            high as my upstairs window.

From inside I follow
         its whirling motions,
the gust so hard
            I can almost hear it.

I follow
         the unpredictable breathing
as wind rises and presses
            into the lush green –

First the small outer leaves
         then the whole body quivering,
and just as suddenly
            a tree so still.

Yesterday I heard a woman
         who wants to return
as a bird. Not because it can soar
            but for its courage.

I'd have chosen
         a tree instead,
tall and thick-rooted,
            near water or stone.

No wings needed
      to remember
the brush of wind
       through my hair,

Or the shift
      of heat and cold
on my shoulders,
       the terrible thirst before rain.

A tree knows
      the longing that's heard
in each wind, the silence
      of one leaf falling.

Balm of Memory

I'll always know the perfume
of warm Sierra Madre afternoons
today's spring air spiked
with the same thick piquant
a little like lemon or mint
though sticky and sometimes
too fragrant to bear
the name eucalyptus
coming after the fact
it was smell, sweet smell
I unwittingly saved
on the walk home from school.

I don't recall being unhappy
but my love for sad trees
their long arms and leaves so slender
began with the silhouette and scent
of the pepper trees shading
Grove Street and Mariposa Avenue
back then the tiniest slight
could make me cry
I was raised to smile
keep yearnings to myself
I watched how the lightest of breezes
could arouse the willowy green
of the fernlike pepper
and how I'd catch
my breath for pretty things
that felt so good in the eye.

This was my life before I started
before I referred to trees
as miracles to cherish
in my spare time — a city girl
who took so much from nature
not ever suspecting
what seeds were taking root —
to store the lavender blue
of jacaranda, my footsteps cushioned
by so many fallen blossoms
or sound out *syc-a-more,*
lau-rel, and *ju-ni-per,* names
that charmed me
for no special reason
as I took in each tree's aroma
like a promise.

Singularity

each leaf inside it dreaming
Lorca

/ eucalyptus

to harbor
this ceiling
of slender
leaf

no wind
but a girl's
lingering
breath

still
unknowing
the body
stirs

/ bamboo

new spring shoots
in green profusion

delighted, the eye
captures a tiny sprig

the hand becoming
each bamboo leaf

brushstrokes
on a sturdy stem

one by one
light & quick

/ pine

sky-born, I enter —
the wind is colder here
cloudmist & fog
wrapping me
in their graceful shawl

no dream of falling
to this bed of needles
warm & fragrant
a sound of footsteps
in my ear

/ Japanese maple

slow blaze
inside the delicate
scarlet branch

I want to remember
warm August nights
cricket chirp & the echo
of laughter

9

Nagatsuki Long Month

Autumn

lately she is looking too much at the moon, especially now that her body has grown so silent, even too reasonable as it calms what wells up inside and used to scream, from rage or minor distress, no matter but the decisiveness of that noise, such ferocious and lunatic release of a woman wailing like a she-wolf, especially on those moon-filled nights to weep as if the pain would never go away. how surprised that she misses those monthly bewitchings, the lunar waters rising so deep inside her, the belly thickening and breasts so tender. what name to call this body now?

II

she wants to find herself
a woman's calendar
one that doesn't need
thirteen moons
to govern the year

an almanac for women like her
whose wombs have been taken
by age or by force
bodies that no longer warn
with the certainty of tides

III

she's heading east in this early morning traffic
      the sky a haze of pale pinks and blues
            rounding a curve something luminous follows

                    she can feel her heart racing
                         knows that looking behind can be dangerous
        but she turns to see the moon resting
                                        on the western horizon
                    keeps her eye on the stranded
                                    full moon in her rearview mirror

        IV

*driving home, she can't stop gazing through her windshield — the night
sky brighter than she's ever seen. she hurries back to him so they can
watch together, sighting stars that are usually hidden above the city. she
hopes he'll embrace her as he used to — but he doesn't. how grateful when
her heart only drops for an instant, then soaring into darkness, she
returns to that ripe old moon, so ablaze with heavy promise.*

Unexpected Passage

Mine was tilted, the doctor told me,
when I gave birth. It was the first time
I'd heard my uterus described. How
a tilted uterus, or even a normal one, looks
remains a mystery – mine
had to be cut out.
Not because of its odd position.
It just never cooperated, growing
scar tissue like weeds taking over a field.

I wish I'd seen it upon removal.
Did it seem lopsided? Was it bloody?
Warm to the touch? It was once big enough
to carry my son safely, the birth waters protecting
him even during a car accident,
my body slamming against the dashboard.
Now, just days after surgery, I still don't miss
the uterus that once amazed me.
For too long it's given me nothing
but messy, unpredictable periods, countless
stained bedsheets and nightgowns,
my monthly dread of embarrassing puddles
made public before family and friends.

I can't decide whether to celebrate or cry.
For thirty-five years I took it all for granted –
never questioned my fertility, the female
power to grow a child inside me.
I want to claim this round,
empty belly I've become.

More than ever before I need to believe
the old woman who dances with me,
know that her voice has always been mine,
now echoing through this womb,
eggs gone, finally
empty.

To Know Her

from a Manuel Alvarez Bravo photograph

Let me see her more closely
this woman walking before me naked
with the sun on her back a forest of palms surrounding
the leaves lit in slivers of white to illuminate the generous body
a thickening torso still defined by a womb
that no longer gives eggs.

Let me walk like her in the afternoon's glare knowing I am the same
a woman who's bled her own small ocean this body
whose skin has torn and stretched the imprint of
birth scars woven forever to the belly
and whose breasts once heavy with milk
now rest low on the ribs.

Let me marvel at such fullness at the substance and curve
the sun searing its heat into breasts
their shadows reflected on midriff and waist
and the warm light that grows
narrow from the chest then widening to hips
held in a radiant triangle.

Red Sky

from *Chagall's* Les Amants au ciel rouge
(Lovers in the Red Sky)

Possibility

Only a sky so red could hold
all the blood which has left
the woman's body, all that
her womb didn't use.

She lies naked in this red sky,
which has also become her bed.
She bares her breasts, the only reminder
of a ripeness she no longer bears.

Her arms won't be broken
from the circle they make
round the bodiless head
of the woman she carries.

Her arms won't open
for the man who brings flowers
but appears to be holding them
just beyond her reach.

In her sleep the light is too red.
And under her closed lids
a red bird hovers
in the corner of her dreams.

The Stain

Now she dresses in white
sleeps in white silk
veils hips and legs
in a long sheer skirt

The sky is always red for a woman who keeps waking
to the flapping of wings, a rush of warm air,
that familiar smell of blood just released —
how heavy the ache in her emptying womb.
But tonight she recalls a sensation of flying
when she floats inside her own body
breathing a liquid rhythm.
She wonders if this is what the dying know —
this lightness after the blood stills —
how dense with red must her sky become
for a woman to grow out of desire.

She wants to be taken again and again
even higher the next time
she will stain the sky red
with so much yearning held in

10

Kannatsuki Godless Month

During this month all the gods gather at the Izumo shrine in Shimane.

Beyond Simple Counting

watching film coverage of the bombing of the
Kurdish minority in Iraq

Hardly anyone sees the rain of mustard gas
once the canisters explode
in a town that nobody's heard of.

Many of the bodies are found chemically frozen –
women clutching infants at the second of impact,
two lovers embracing, their last
human gesture preserved.

Other victims are burnt beyond simple counting,
though hundreds of bodies share long earthen trenches
hastily dug for the crowded anonymous.

It can be worse for the permanently wounded
who still aren't sure they've survived the bombing –
the woman whose insanity can't be traced
to the toxic fumes or a memory that won't die,
the man in his twenties whose spine's curving protrusion
prevents him from standing, his future contorted
to lie prone on his stomach forever.

How long can a deadly gas be trapped underground,
the once-fertile soil too contaminated for seed?
How diffused is the poison that penetrates skin?
No known cure for the genetically altered –
these men without sperm in their semen,
these mothers whose poisoned babies
will pass on the mutant cells
in a litany of names no one hears.

After

September 11, 2001

no words now
just eyes
nothing more to say, god
just eyes

to tell us more
than we can bear
only eyes, god
nothing less

only eyes
once the sky became too bare
no eyes but these
to see, god

nothing
save the sky in these red eyes
whose sky, god
whose

Toward a Defining Gesture

not the upraised arms
that point straight to heaven
not the emptied palms
with fingers outspread

> *but hands silently*
> *tendered from*
> *the kneeling body*
> *palms pressed*
> *together, the light*
> *bow of forehead*
> *and lips to*
> *a grace of fingers*

not the limbs sent skyward
sinewed branches, even twigs
bearing the impossible weight
of so much blossoming leaf

> *but the bony, knobbed arms*
> *always clasping*
> *the ground*
> *roots that twist*
> *and rise*
> *from the stem*
> *while tunneling so long*
> *in the dark*

The Flowering Eye

but if you want beauty
you've got to fight for it

Mbembe Milton Smith

You think these pretties come easy but you don't
even want to know how tired the cry
until there's so much
craze and stark the world
begins to bleed in places no one dares imagine
not even stone
or the one we call God
can remember a more terrifying time.

And maybe that's part of the secret
this dangerous promise binding
each of us who stumble into a moment
so ravishing we become
eternally intoxicated
like the dumbstruck lover always
longing for one more look
no matter how fleeting just one
last delicious gasp for
the shimmer and hum we so stubbornly pursue.

No killing field too big for our exquisite need
we strum in the gorgeous looming
so near the latest ragged assault
and oh how incredible
the beauty we'll win
at such unforgiving cost.

⌒

What shade of green
for a man who still holds the paintbrush
clenched between his teeth
after the limbs no longer move
and the fingers betray.

What word chosen by a man who's lost
every muscle but the nerve in his eye
which can follow a tiny beam
of light locking on
each individual letter
until he builds a word into a sentence
into a world that's willing
to read him.

⌒

The bombing won't stop but we're not as fragile as we fear
especially when those faces of anguish an ocean away
can be switched on and off with the evening news
the stage cleared away for a feast of orchids
hundreds in April bloom as we
gorge ourselves on the delicate hues
the stillness of moving water nearby.

All through the war we'll be patient as gardeners
cultivate a memory that can blossom at spring.

11

Shimotsuki Month of Frost

Winter Garden

Inside, this light
is so lean —
each dry branch
a pale brown line,
my fingers also
slender like twigs.
I've kept desert flowers
in my bedroom,
removed them
from a winter's wind.
When rearranged
a few more white blossoms
fall, here
on the darker
ground of my hand,
new snow.

A Gift of Iris in Winter: Improvisations

I

I haven't told you how impossible it's becoming,
or how dangerously you hang
on the lingering thread
of my own hesitation —
you bring me these slender stalks of iris,
the buds just about to open,
and you don't even notice
me pulling you back in.

II

Tonight you offer
your hands,
if only for seconds.
You carefully cut
the iris stems,
placing them
in a narrow
glass vase,
then a few sprigs
of baby's breath
and just enough water
before beckoning me
to admire.

III

There's no word in my dictionary
to capture the exact shade of iris in winter —
fuller than lilac or lavender,
bluer than hyacinth, but distinct
from fuchsia, plum, or wine —
the subtle modulations
between purple and violet
that can only be recorded
with the naked eye.

IV

After two days the buds have opened —
no evidence of the painter who's brushed
a quick stroke of yellow on each dark petal,
that genius who dares
tamper with beauty
in such wild imperfection.

V

How well I know
this particular hue —
it belongs to that memory
of a woman who died
before I could really get to know her,
leaving a lace-covered gown
the same ivory of baby's breath,
photographs long removed
from their dressy frames,
the bride's bouquet of iris
in a bed of white gardenias.

VI

As the iris
opens
a sigh rises up
in me. Your
sigh comes
from another
place, so far
away from
your body,
so very far
from mine.

Asymmetry

This twenty-year avocado tree
leans too much to the east
as if it has always strained
to find enough water and light,
yet so many young avocados —
an unexpected winter harvest
growing from its crooked branches.
Like my Japanese ancestors, I've learned
to embrace the nonsymmetric,
that imperfection so necessary
to unlock the tree's secret buttery taste,
a delicious mystery no matter how decrepit
its trunk and limbs —
and I dare to ask what new fruit
wait to be discovered
even from an old aching body like mine.

12

Shiwasu Month of the Running Teacher

This is a busy month for teachers of tea ceremony and flower arrangement.

Presence

Old monk sits in a garden
made of nothing but stones
a garden without
the distractions
of ginkgo or flowering
cherry trees
no bursts of purple
from iris or eggplant
no pond brimming
with pollywogs, lotus
and vermilion koi
just ordinary stones
a man can carry
from the sea
choosing
smooth, dark ovals
of charcoal and raven,
ebony, carbon and ink

Sometimes he
sweeps them
with the soft bristles
of a bamboo broom

Sometimes rain
washes them
water clinging
to the stones' thirsty skins
now reflected by sun
in this glistening ground

Every night
old monk listens
to an abundant stillness
giving thanks

Hints for Beginning Algebra Students

*(also aspiring carpenters, poets,
and rock climbers)*

I. *to solve any equation*

find the value of the unknown
look all around
figure out which of the billion
things you don't understand
is the one question *you*
have to know
no matter how long
or far it takes

maybe you want to grow a sweeter
strawberry or put a smile back
on the face of your eight-year-old son

come join this ancient fraternity
all failing students
dying to decipher
the grand dance of lights
in the northern night sky
or lightning bugs
or just plain love

II. *adding to one side requires subtracting from the other*

how tempting to tip the scales. too much vinegar or bliss.
greed as it cracks the luminous lens.

shake in sugar and salt till the tongue cannot detect
the part from the whole. taste new and delicious alchemies.

think of a painter's palette — squeezing more red
may call for watering down blue. week after week,
a patient brush can stroke all 9,000 shades of green.

III. *to isolate the unknown variable, simplify*

this is harder than it sounds
as you squeeze your clutter close to breast.
the piles and closets of noisy necessities
making it hazardous
to cross the living room,
impossible to hear the emptiness
your heart so longs for.

it can be downright suicidal,
cutting out those false eyes, limbs, mouths
that charm and disarm you,
insane to desert the things
that have your name stamped on them.

but like the monk on stone mountain,
know how much more
is less.

IV. *when the equation has no answer*

it is called the null set
nothing works
mother of all dilemmas

some resort to prayer
others fill their beaks with honey
at hummingbird speed

welcome to this mystery

v. *when the equation is yes, no matter what*

it remains true
through every bombing
always so
through each new outrage

every voice joined
in heart's infinite call
just one more breath
the moistened eye opens
a sky so blue it never ends

Stone, Bow, Prayer

from a news story about the continuing
tradition of Japanese archers who,
blindfolded, shoot arrows into mounds
of hay, which I call the "grass mountain";
and from seeing Mexican divers in Acapulco
leap toward invisible targets

Let me hear
the clarity of stone,
one small enough
to hold, its cool
singular weight
in my warm hand.

Let me lay stone
in still water, on white
sand or paper —
the only adornment
I need
to give me this
place I look out from,
to speak my own
simple name.

      ↩

I am a patient
archer, aiming
these arrows blindly
into the grass mountain —
believing
I'm landing each dart

even closer, enclosing
an unseeable center.

        ∽

At night I wait for a sign
in the wind, a stillness
in the cold, black water
before jumping
from the rocky ledge,
knowing my body must
find its way through darkness.
I begin each dive like the first time—
a whispered invocation.

        ∽

I cannot deny
this persistence
to want the heart
of things to shine—
barely one sound.

Balancing Stones

I have seen
ordinary hands
able to place
one stone upon another
no matter how
different the shapes
or unlikely
the weights

What holds them
together
is some center
invisible to the eye
only realized
when the hands
are patient
and trust is complete

How else
to explain
their creating
stone sculptures
with no nails
or cement
no welding tools
for support

The tip
of a craggy stone
becomes the unlikely
pin able to steady
the heft of a rounder
stone whose surface
is curving
and smooth

On the sloping
top of one shore stone
a second leans without slipping
the third smaller and jagged
then the large oval
to form a tower
undisturbed
by sea breeze

There is a locus
some hands can find
a single point
in the body
to which another
separate body
is gravitationally
attracted

I have seen
such harmony
rooted in the impossible
position of two stones' hearts
no matter how oblique
the angle
one center holding
firmly to the other

About the Author

Amy Uyematsu is a sansei (third-generation Japanese American) from Los Angeles. Winner of the 1992 Nicholas Roerich Poetry Prize, she has two previous volumes of poetry, *30 Miles from J-Town* (Story Line Press, 1992) and *Nights of Fire, Nights of Rain* (Story Line Press, 1998). She was also a co-editor of *Roots: An Asian American Reader* (UCLA Asian American Studies Center Press, 1971), one of the earliest anthologies in Asian American Studies.

The Chinese character for poetry is made up of two parts: "word" and "temple." It also serves as pressmark for Copper Canyon Press. Founded in 1972, Copper Canyon Press remains dedicated to publishing poetry exclusively, from Nobel laureates to new and emerging authors. The Press thrives with the generous patronage of readers, writers, booksellers, librarians, teachers, students, and funders— everyone who shares the conviction that poetry invigorates the language and sharpens our appreciation of the world.

Major funding has been provided by:

The Paul G. Allen Family Foundation

THE **PAUL G. ALLEN FAMILY** *foundation*

Lannan Foundation

Lannan

National Endowment for the Arts

The Starbucks Foundation

NATIONAL
ENDOWMENT
FOR THE ARTS

Washington State Arts Commission

THE
STARBUCKS
FOUNDATION

For information and catalogs:

COPPER CANYON PRESS
Post Office Box 271
Port Townsend, Washington 98368
360-385-4925
www.coppercanyonpress.org

Set in Mendoza, a typeface designed by José Mendoza y Almeida. Book design and composition by Valerie Brewster, Scribe Typography. Printed on archival-quality paper.

CPSIA information can be obtained at www.ICGtesting.com
Printed in the USA
LVOW11s0502130916

504230LV00007B/18/P